ISBN 978-1-934655-25-2

06-031 • COPYRIGHT © 2005 **World Evangelism Press**®
P.O. Box 262550 • Baton Rouge, Louisiana 70826-2550
Website: www.jsm.org • Email: info@jsm.org
225-768-7000

TABLE OF CONTENTS

How The Holy Spirit Works

The Cross Of Christ Series

Introduction

HOW THE HOLY SPIRIT WORKS

INTRODUCTION

The material that we hope to give you in this Volume, as simple as it will be, is, I feel, some of the most important material that you will ever read. I can say that because I am not promoting myself, but rather the illumination the Holy Spirit has given me, as it regards the Word of God, as to how the Holy Spirit works.

To know how He does what He does, and why He does it, considering that He is God, presents itself as illumination of unprecedented proportions.

And yet, what we will give you is not something new. It adds nothing to the Word of God, and it certainly does not delete anything from the Word of God. It is illumination on the Word that was already given to the Apostle Paul, which He then gave to us in his Epistles.

PENTECOSTALS AND CHARISMATICS

The Church as a whole is woefully deficient as it regards knowledge concerning the Holy Spirit. Pentecostals (and I am Pentecostal) and Charismatics at times boast about knowledge concerning the Spirit of God, but, truthfully, beyond speaking with other tongues, and a little knowledge about the Gifts of the Spirit, that's about the extent of what is known and understood even by those who claim to know.

I would pray that the information given in this short Volume will be widely disseminated, understood, believed, and taken to one's self, for I believe that is what the Lord intends.

To know how the Holy Spirit works, at least as much as a poor human being can know, presents itself as illumination of unprecedented proportions. If we are able to add to your knowledge regarding this all-important subject, then our efforts will be worthwhile. To be sure, such knowledge, which has been, and is, imparted by the Holy Spirit, could only be given by Revelation. As stated, it is Revelation concerning the Word already given.

REVELATION

When we speak of Revelation, we are simply meaning that the Holy Spirit gives one the illumination on a particular Passage of Scripture, or else a particular subject related in the Word of God. Anything given by the Lord will always be perfectly according to the Word of God, never adding to the Word, and never taking from the Word.

I think we will prove adequately that what we will attempt to give you will be exactly according to the Word of God.

As all true Revelation regarding the Scripture, we find from our study that such is progressive. In other words, it is ever the desire of the Lord to lead His Church deeper into the Word, with the Church learning more as the Holy Spirit reveals it to us.

The Word of God is absolutely inexhaustible. No matter how much one learns about it, there is more to be learned, actually a great deal more! That's why Paul referred to the Word as *"The Everlasting Covenant"* (Heb. 13:20).

This means that the Word of God, i.e., *"The New Covenant,"* will never have to be amended in any fashion. It is perfect and, therefore, complete exactly as it is. That is one of the reasons that I am alarmed at the plethora of paraphrases and interpretations of the Word of God which are coming on the market, such as the Message Bible, etc. If your Bible is not a word-for-word translation, such as the King James, then it is not a reliable representation of the Word of God, but is rather something else entirely.

Jesus said, *"Man shall not live by bread alone, but by every Word that proceeds out of the Mouth of God"* (Mat. 4:4).

While translations themselves, no matter how accurate, definitely are not inspired, still, the efforts of the Hebrew and Greek Scholars attempting to arrive at a translation which is as close as possible to the original Hebrew or Greek Texts is the only thing that can be deemed acceptable. Those who would accept anything else definitely are not wise!

THE OFFICE WORK OF THE HOLY SPIRIT

Every single thing done on this Earth by the Godhead, with one exception, has always been carried out by the Person, the Office, and the Ministry of the Holy Spirit. His Work began with the renovation of the Earth; the Scripture says, *"And the Spirit of God moved upon the face of the waters"* (Gen. 1:2). As someone has well said, *"The Moving and Operation of the Holy Spirit signals the beginning of life."* And without that Moving and Operation, there is no life!

The one thing the Holy Spirit did not carry out on this Earth, as it pertains to the Godhead, was the price paid by the Lord Jesus Christ at Calvary's Cross. Even then, the Holy Spirit functioned in every capacity of the Master's Life and Ministry.

Jesus' conception in the womb of the Virgin Mary was by the decree of the Holy Spirit (Mat. 1:18). When Jesus began His earthly Ministry, it was the Spirit of God Who energized and anointed Christ for this all-important work (Mat. 3:16).

As His Ministry began, it was the Spirit of God Who led Jesus into the wilderness *"to be tempted of the Devil"* (Mat. 4:1).

Not long after He began His Ministry, He stood in the Synagogue of His hometown of Nazareth and said, *"The Spirit of the Lord is upon Me, because He has anointed Me to preach the Gospel to the poor; He has sent Me to heal the brokenhearted, to preach deliverance to the captives, and recovering of sight to the blind, to set at liberty them who are bruised, to preach the acceptable year of the Lord"* (Lk. 4:18-19). In fact, when Jesus died on the Cross, it was the Holy Spirit Who told Him the very moment that He could die (Heb. 9:14). As well, it was the Holy Spirit Who raised Christ from the dead (Rom. 8:11).

Just before His Ascension, the last Message that Christ gave to His followers, and even His closest Disciples, was the necessity of them first of all being Baptized with the Holy Spirit.

"And, being assembled together with them, Commanded them that they should not depart from Jerusalem, but wait for the Promise of the Father, which said He, You have heard of Me.

"For John truly baptized with water; but you shall be baptized with the Holy Spirit not many days hence" (Acts 1:4-5).

His statement to them was not a suggestion, but rather a command. He was telling them, *"Do not go preach, do not go teach, do not go do anything for Me, until you first are baptized with the Holy Spirit."*

8

As God, Jesus needed no anointing of the Spirit, as should be obvious; however, as Man (for it was as Man that He functioned), He needed the Holy Spirit for everything He did. And so do we!

THE NECESSITY OF THE HOLY SPIRIT

Let me say again what I have just stated:

If Jesus, Who was the Son of the Living God, Who was God manifest in the flesh, Who was the Creator of all things, and Who was the Redeemer of all mankind, at least all who will believe, needed the Operation of the Holy Spirit within His Life and Ministry, where does that leave us?

Although Christ is the Source and the Cross is the Means for every single thing done in our hearts and lives for God, it is the Holy Spirit Who superintends the doing of all things. In other words, whatever is done, He must do it, or else it is not done.

THE HOLY SPIRIT WILL BLESS ONLY
THAT WHICH HE CONCEIVES

Fallen man cannot produce anything, at least that which God will honor and bless. So that means that anything that God does on this Earth, and I mean anything and everything, must first of all be conceived by the Holy Spirit. If it is not conceived and birthed by the Holy Spirit, then God cannot bless it. It is just that simple!

That's the reason that every Believer must be filled with the Spirit, must be led by the Spirit, must be guided by the Spirit, must be empowered by the Spirit and, thereby, must seek the Lord constantly that the Holy Spirit will have His Way within our hearts and lives. Sadly, virtually everything being done in the field of religion was conceived by man, and not the Lord. Therefore, in the final analysis, no matter how much religious machinery is attached, it will accomplish nothing for the Lord. The Lord will only bless that which He Himself conceives.

The Revelation that I will give you in this short Volume was given to me by the Lord. It was conceived by the Lord and given birth by the Lord. Therefore, I know that if faith will be evidenced regarding that which will be given in this short Volume, great blessings will accrue. This which the Lord gave to me was not only for me, but is meant for the entirety of the Church. That I know beyond the shadow of a doubt!

Will it be received by all?

Nothing of the Lord is ever received by all. In the final analysis, only a few will receive it. The Scripture plainly tells us, *"Few there be who find it"* (Mat. 7:14). But of the *"few"* who really do find this of which we speak, their lives will be gloriously and wondrously changed, and changed so much for the better.

Chapter 1

The Holy Spirit

CHAPTER ONE

THE HOLY SPIRIT

Even though the subject matter of this book is not necessarily the Baptism with the Holy Spirit, yet I feel that a short dissertation must be given regarding this all-important aspect of the Believer's life and living.

The first recollection I have of the Holy Spirit concerns something that transpired between my Mother and my Dad as it regarded my Grandmother. I was eight years old. The year was 1943.

It was the summer months, and I was not in school. One morning after I arose, I went into the Living Room, where my Mother and my Dad were standing beside my piano discussing my Dad's Mother, i.e., my Grandmother. I always referred to my Grandmother as *"Nannie."* At a very tender age, I had tried to pronounce *"Grannie,"* but couldn't. Instead I came up with *"Nannie,"* and the name stuck.

I stopped to listen to what my Mother and Dad were discussing in connection with my Grandmother, because the topic captivated my interest.

"Mama has gone crazy over religion," I heard my Dad say!

My Mother joined in by saying, *"Ever since she came back from that Campmeeting, she speaks in some kind of funny language, and that's all she talks about day and night."*

My parents, my Grandmother, and some others of my relatives all attended the same Church. But since our little Church was relatively new, the subject of the Baptism with the Holy Spirit, with the evidence of speaking with other tongues, had not yet been broached too very much. My parents actually did not know anything about the Holy Spirit. They both thought my Grandmother was being fanatical.

Even though they were speaking in a negative manner about my Grandmother, still, it did not strike me that way. I wanted to know what they were talking about, so I jumped on my bicycle and immediately rode to my Grandmother's house. I will never forget the scene which then transpired.

THE POWER OF GOD

My Grandmother was in the kitchen, preparing a cup of hot tea. I said to her, *"Nannie, Mama and Daddy say that you have received something at a Campmeeting that makes you speak funny. What are they talking about?"*

I will never forget her reaction. She laughed and said, *"Jimmy, just as soon as I fix this hot tea, I will tell you all about it."*

Momentarily, she came into the Living Room and sat down, placing the cup of hot tea on a little table beside her. I sat down on the floor, Indian-fashion, looking up at her. Then she began to tell me how the Lord had baptized her with the Holy Spirit with the evidence of speaking with other tongues. As stated, this was the first time, at least that I could recall, that I had heard anything about the Holy Spirit, much less this great phenomenon.

As my Grandmother began to relate how she had sought the Lord for the Holy Spirit all during the Campmeeting, but still had not received, she then came to the part where the Lord filled her. She told of the hunger and the thirst that was so acute that she felt she would die if she did not experience the Baptism with the Holy Spirit.

That morning, they had service under the Tabernacle, but my Grandmother still was not filled. The lunch hour came, and she told a few lady friends that she was not interested in lunch, because she wanted to go out under a cope of trees and continue to seek for the Holy Spirit. Several other ladies went with her.

She left the Tabernacle because many were eating their lunches there and she did not want to disturb them.

As my Grandmother began to seek the Lord, and others began to pray with her, all of a sudden the Spirit of God came upon her and she began to speak with other tongues as the Spirit of God gave the utterance. The moment she came to that part in her story, the power of God hit her, and, at the same time, it also hit me. Even though I had been saved a few weeks earlier, this was the first time that I had seriously felt the Presence and the Power of God.

I remember it running all over me just like someone had poured water over me. I looked down at my arms to see that chill bumps had broken out because of this phenomenon.

My Grandmother threw up her hands and began to speak with other tongues. As stated, I felt what she felt, even though I did not receive at that time. However, I would never be the same again. I had sensed and felt the Power of God, and nothing else would ever satisfy.

I went back again that afternoon and had my Grandmother tell me the same story all over again. In fact, I went back every day, some days as many as three times, to get her to tell me the same story, because I knew that when she got to that place about being filled, the Power of God would hit her, and it would also roll over on me.

That was my initiation to the Baptism with the Holy Spirit.

MY PERSONAL BAPTISM

We started having prayer meetings, as many as two a day, and I grew so hungry for the Holy Spirit during that time. It was at a prayer meeting at our Church where the Lord gloriously and wondrously satisfied the hunger of my heart by giving me the same thing that He had given my Grandmother. The Lord Baptized me with the Holy Spirit.

I was kneeling that morning beside the Altar, with my hands uplifted. All of a sudden, the Power of God, which I had sensed so many times the last few days, literally covered my being. And then there was a light that seemed to settle around me, a light that is very difficult for me to explain. It seemed to be liquid light, even though I don't think there is such a thing. But yet that is what it seemed to me to be like. It seemed to settle around me as I began to speak with other tongues as the Spirit of God moved upon me.

For the next several days I spoke in tongues more than I spoke English.

A PERSONAL EXPERIENCE

A few days after I was baptized with the Holy Spirit, my Mother sent me to the Post Office to get a stamp. In those days, if I remember correctly, a first-class stamp cost three cents. At any rate, I walked up to the window, placed the nickel on the counter, and opened my mouth to ask for the stamp, but I began to speak in tongues. To be sure, it was not contrived on my part, it just came out unbidden.

I made another effort, but started speaking in tongues again. The man behind the counter was looking at me strangely. I did not look foreign, but I sure sounded foreign. He said, *"Son, I can't understand what you are saying. Would you please repeat it?"*

I made still another stab at it, and again I began to speak in tongues. By this time, I was frightened myself, so I grabbed my nickel and ran away. When I got to the house, my mother, of course, asked me to give her the stamp. But I had no stamp, and when I tried to tell her what had happened, strangely enough, I could now speak English.

Why the Lord did this, I will never know, but He did!

LOOK WHAT THE LORD
HAS DONE

If I remember correctly, the year was 2002. The Secretary of State for the State of Louisiana had instituted a program where particular individuals were inducted to a Hall of Fame for the purpose of increasing tourism to the State of Louisiana. The same Post Office of which I had just spoken, which was built in the days of the Depression (the 1930's), and which had a very ornamental structure, was turned into a museum. My two cousins, Jerry Lee Lewis and Mickey Gilley, and myself were inducted into the Louisiana Hall of Fame on this particular day. Thousands of people were in the city for this occasion. Mickey was there, but Jerry Lee was not able to attend due to circumstances which arose at the last minute.

At any rate, it was an excellent meeting; the State rolled out the red carpet, and treated us with all manner of kindness and graciousness. I sang a song and so did Mickey!

When the ceremonies were finished, we were taken down into the museum to give interviews, etc., which we did. After a period of time, I walked away from the exhibits and walked to the front of the Post Office, at least what had served as a Post Office for those many years long ago, and stood there for a few moments at the same window where, as a boy, I had stood many times to purchase stamps. But the main reason I stood there is because of the little incident that took place when I was only eight years old.

From that time until now, the Lord has helped us to touch a great part of this world with the Gospel of Jesus Christ, for which we give Him all the praise and all the glory.

LOOKING TO THE HOLY SPIRIT

When I use the heading, *"Looking to the Holy Spirit,"* I mean that only in the sense of depending on Him. We are to look unto Jesus, the Author and the Finisher of our Faith. To be sure, the Holy Spirit will always glorify Christ (Jn. 16:14).

It is Jesus Who has paid the price on Calvary's Cross; therefore, it is Jesus Who must be glorified, which the Holy Spirit always does.

But yet, as stated, we are to ever understand that everything done in our hearts and lives, as it regards the Lord, is always, without exception, carried out by the Holy Spirit (Jn. 7:37-39).

At my Grandmother's knee I learned what the Holy Spirit could do, and I learned to depend on Him for all that was done. It has helped me to touch this world for Christ, literally seeing hundreds of thousands brought to a saving knowledge of the Grace of God.

However, there was one great Work of the Holy Spirit with which I was not acquainted, and did not know. Because of that, untold difficulties and heartache would accrue unto myself. That, in fact, is what this Study Guide is all about.

THE REVELATION OF THE HOLY SPIRIT

Someone has well said, *"Desperation always precedes Revelation."* Whether that is correct or not, regarding the expression *"always,"* I cannot say; but that's exactly the way it happened with me.

It was the month of March in the year 1988. The largest Ministry in the world was in shambles. There was no end to the hurt and the pain, and it was all my fault. But yet, I was perplexed, totally lacking in understanding, and not knowing why.

When one has tried with all of his strength, and has done everything he knows to do to live the life he ought to live, and then he faces the powers of darkness and fails, such is not a very pleasant experience, to say the least.

On this particular day, I stayed home from the office. I had intended to spend the day in prayer, which I often did. As was my custom, I studied the Word for a while that morning, and then, with a heavy heart, went to prayer. There were a thousand questions, and I did not have any answers!

Our houses, Donnie's and ours, are situated on twenty-five acres of land a little bit outside the city limits of Baton Rouge, Louisiana. During those days, I had the habit of walking around the perimeter of the property as I prayed. It afforded privacy and I enjoyed the scenery.

I will never forget where I was at this particular time. I was at the very back of the property standing near a fence. I suppose I had been seeking the Lord for ten or fifteen minutes.

Without warning, the powers of Satan came over me to such an extent that I had never previously known. It was one of the most powerful attacks I had ever experienced.

The Evil One began to prod me, saying, *"You've disgraced your family, your Church, and those who trusted you, and you've done great harm to the Work of God."* Continuing to push at me harder and harder, he then went on to say, *"Why don't you just disappear. You will do the Work of God a service by just simply getting lost."*

How long this went on, I do not exactly know; however, this I do know: Five minutes of such oppression by the powers of darkness seem like a lifetime.

I remember leaning up against the fence and crying to the Lord, *"You told us that You would not allow anything to be placed on us any harder than we could bear. But no human being can stand this. Please help me!"*

As I have already said, I don't really know how long Satan was allowed to continue this effort, but to me it seemed like a lifetime. But then, all of a sudden it happened!

The oppressive powers of darkness immediately left and were immediately replaced by the Power of God.

THE MOVING OF THE HOLY SPIRIT

One moment it seemed like there was a thousand pounds on my back, and the next moment it seemed like I was floating, with my feet not even touching the ground. The Spirit of God covered me that morning, and, after a period of time, the Lord began to speak to my heart.

He said, *"I am going to show you things about the Holy Spirit that you do not now know."*

I knew this was the Lord; of that I had no doubt. But what exactly did He mean?

The Holy Spirit is God! Consequently, there obviously are many things about the Holy Spirit I don't know; however, I instinctively knew that the Lord was speaking of my dilemma. But yet, at that moment, nothing else was forthcoming. Only the words, *"I am going to show you things about the Holy Spirit that you do not now know."*

I knew the Lord had spoken to me, but yet there was no answer as to what it was — only the prediction of what would be done.

To be sure, the dark times did not end that day. There were several years of heartache, which words cannot even begin to describe. But even though the prediction was there, the Lord never related anything else, as it regards the Holy Spirit.

As stated, that was in 1988. It would be 1997 before the Lord would fulfill this prediction — nine long years!

WHY DID IT TAKE SO LONG?

I suppose I have asked myself that same question any number of times. During that intervening nine years, when it seemed as if the answer would never come, I would cry to the Lord, *"Why?"*

I knew the Lord had spoken to my heart on that day in March, 1988; however, nothing had happened since to fulfill that prediction. I had absolutely no inkling about what the Lord would show me or tell me! I just knew what He had said.

At one point, in the year 1992 (if I remember the year correctly), I became somewhat depressed. In October of 1991, the Lord had instructed me to begin two prayer meetings a day, which we instantly did, a regimen which I personally maintain unto this hour. For a period of time, I asked the Lord why it was taking so long. To be frank, I had grown discouraged.

After several weeks of this, I laid it to rest in my mind, and sought the Lord about other things.

Then one particular night in one of the prayer meetings, it happened. The Lord spoke to my heart and said:

THE REASON FOR THE DELAY

"You have asked Me why it is taking so long. This is My answer to you:

"For precept must be upon precept, precept upon precept; line upon line, line upon line; here a little, and there a little" (Isa. 28:10).

As the Lord gave me this, His Presence filled my heart. I knew it was the Lord, and I knew that He had spoken to me, but what did it all mean?

I had come to understand that He was saying two things to me that night.

First of all, He was saying that the Word of God must be interpreted correctly in all things. There must not be any misunderstanding of the Word.

"Precept must be upon precept, precept upon precept; line upon line, line upon line."

When the Lord says something, of course, it is very important. When He says it twice, it becomes much more important. When He says it four times, even as He did here, then it becomes something of overwhelming significance, as should be abundantly obvious!

As stated, He was telling me that the Word of God must be understood correctly, must be interpreted correctly, and must be held correctly. This much was absolutely imperative.

Second, He was telling me that this was happening *"here a little, and there a little."* Even though it does not take the Lord any time to do anything, it takes us quite a bit of time to be prepared for what the Lord wants to do.

The answer the Lord gave me regarding the lapse of time encouraged me greatly. But there still was no answer regarding that which He had promised.

"I will show you things about the Holy Spirit that you do not now know!"

Over and over again, I pondered over exactly what that might mean, but for nine years there was no answer, at least no definitive answer.

THE REVELATION OF THE CROSS

I wish I could remember the exact day, even the week or the month, but I don't. I do remember that it was in 1997, and, to be frank, there has been some discussion even about the year. But by investigating certain indicators, we have come to the conclusion that 1997 was the year.

I had gone to the office early that morning, which was my habit. This was immediately before I would go on the air for the daily Radio Program, *"A Study In The Word"*.

Among other things that morning, I was working on the Commentary to Paul's Epistle to the Romans. I had come to the Sixth Chapter. As I was studying this particular Chapter, and realizing that this is one of the most important Chapters in the entirety of the Word of God, the Lord began to open up to me the cause of all the problems I had experienced.

I've given this account in other Volumes, so I won't go into detail here.

That morning He showed me that the problem was the sin nature. He showed me that my lack of understanding of the sin nature and how it is to be addressed was the cause of all my problems. When the Lord explained this to me, I cannot even begin to tell you how I felt. As I have already stated, when one tries so very, very hard, and then fails, this leaves one very confused.

Why?

Now I knew the answer to that question. I knew why!

But yet, that morning the Lord did not tell me the solution to the problem, only what the problem was.

**THE ANSWER FOR WHICH YOU SEEK
IS THE CROSS OF CHRIST**

Several mornings later in one of our prayer meetings, I was thanking the Lord for what He had shown me, because I knew that it was so very, very important, when, all of a sudden, the Spirit of God began to move upon me again.

The Lord then gently spoke to my heart:

"The answer for which you seek is the Cross of Christ."

Then He said it again:

"The solution for which you seek is the Cross of Christ, and the Cross of Christ alone!"

Once again, He took me to the Sixth Chapter of Romans, Verses 3-5.

Of course, that was just the beginning. Again, I cannot tell you how I felt. I knew the problem, and now I knew the solution to that problem. It was, and is, the Cross of Christ!

From that time until now, a period of some years, the Lord has continued to open up to me this great Truth regarding the Cross as given to us in the Sixth Chapter of Romans.

I rejoiced greatly in what the Lord had thus far given unto me, and I knew it was the answer to my dilemma, but then I began to wonder what part the Holy Spirit played in all of this. I knew He played a great part, but, at that time, I did not understand what that part was. I knew it was all completed at the Cross; so, if it was all done at the Cross, where does this leave the Holy Spirit?

Regarding my question, I sought the Lord for an answer, but no answer came immediately. Actually, during that period of time, the prediction the Lord had made to me in 1988 never really crossed my mind. It had been so long that I rarely thought upon it any more. And yet, I knew that although what the Lord had given me about the Cross was wonderful beyond compare, it really was not the entirety of what I should know. Instinctively, I felt this, but I never linked it with the Promise the Lord had made to me back in 1988.

I kept praying about it, asking the Lord to show me the part as to how the Holy Spirit played into all of this. To be sure, whenever one prays in that manner, totally sincere of heart, desiring to know what the Lord wants us to know, this is a prayer that will always be answered.

Several weeks went by. As the Lord began to open up to me the Message of the Cross, I immediately began to teach what little I did know over our daily Radio Program, *"A Study In The Word"*.

I don't exactly remember if we were in the Sixth Chapter of Romans or the Eighth Chapter. But whatever Chapter it was, I was teaching on the Cross.

THE FULFILLMENT OF THE PROMISE

If I remember correctly, that day only Loren Larson was with me on the Program. As I began teaching, I made statements that I had never before even contemplated. I said:

"The Holy Spirit works entirely within the framework of the Finished Work of Christ, and He will not work outside of that framework."

I remember that as I said those words, I somewhat surprised myself, because I had not previously thought on the subject, I had not contemplated that subject, and I actually had stated something that I didn't even previously know. But I knew that what I had stated was of the Lord, and that it was Biblical, and I knew that it was correct. It was, in fact, a tremendous Truth!

THE HOLY SPIRIT WORKS ONLY WITHIN THE FRAMEWORK OF THE CROSS OF CHRIST

This is a great Truth that the majority of the Church do not know, and, in fact, have no idea whatsoever as to what it means.

The idea is this:

Whatever the Holy Spirit does, it is the Cross which gives Him the legal means to carry out the task, and I am speaking of that which He does in the hearts and lives of Believers.

As stated, the Holy Spirit is the One Who carries out the directions of the Godhead. One might say that He is the Mechanic. This involves everything; however, when it comes to Believers, He works entirely within the framework of the Finished Work of Christ, and only within that framework. And I will prove it in just a moment.

AN OLD TESTAMENT ILLUSTRATION

Before I conclude telling about what the Lord did for me that day, please allow me to take you to the Old Testament, which will also verify this of which I speak. (In a moment, I will give a more definitive explanation from the New Testament.)

Concerning the consecration of the Priests and the Sacrifice, the Scripture says, *"And he slew it; and Moses took of the blood of it, and put it upon the tip of Aaron's right ear, and upon the thumb of his right hand, and upon the great toe of his right foot.*

"And he brought Aaron's sons, and Moses put of the blood of the tip of their right ear, and upon the thumbs of their right hands, and upon the great toes of their right feet: and Moses sprinkled the blood upon the Altar round about" (Lev. 8:23-24).

Of course, the Sacrifice being killed and the blood of the Sacrifice being applied at it was to Aaron and his sons, all who were Priests, signified the Cross and what Jesus there would do in order to redeem fallen humanity.

Then the Scripture says, *"And Moses took of the anointing oil, and of the blood which was upon the Altar, and sprinkled it upon Aaron, and upon his garments, and upon his sons, and upon his sons' garments with him; and sanctified Aaron and his garments, and his sons, and his sons' garments with him"* (Lev. 8:30).

The blood was applied first and then the *"anointing oil"*; the latter was a Type of the Holy Spirit, again portraying the fact that the Holy Spirit works entirely within the framework of the Finished Work of Christ.

Again, as it regards the cleansing of the leper, the Scripture says:

"The Priest shall take some of the blood of the Trespass Offering, and the Priest shall put it upon the tip of the right ear of him who is to be cleansed, and upon the thumb of his right hand, and upon the great toe of his right foot:

"And the Priest shall take some of the log of oil, and pour it into the palm of his own left hand:

"And the Priest shall dip his right finger in the oil that is in his left hand, and shall sprinkle of the oil with his finger seven times before the LORD:

"And of the rest of the oil that is in his hand shall the Priest put upon the tip of the right ear of him who is to be cleansed, and upon the thumb of his right hand, and upon the great toe of his right foot, and upon the blood of the Trespass Offering" (Lev. 14:14-17).

Again we see that the oil, which is a Type of the Holy Spirit, was not applied until the blood had first been applied, portraying the fact that the Holy Spirit works exclusively within the framework of the Cross, at least as it refers to Believers. The Holy Spirit does nothing but that it is done strictly by and through what Christ did at the Cross.

To be sure, everything done in Old Testament times occurred before the Cross; however, it was done *"on credit,"* one might say. This means that whatever action was taken by the Holy Spirit was done with the idea that the Redeemer is coming, and that one day the Cross would be an accomplished fact, which it was!

ROMANS 8:2

That day, as I sat there behind the desk teaching the people over Radio, I had made the statement, *"The Holy Spirit works exclusively within the framework of the Finished Work of Christ, and He will work in no other way."*

As stated, it surprised me somewhat when I said it, because it was not a statement that I knew or understood. I had not premeditated the statement, had not even thought of such, and nothing like that was even on my mind.

So, I knew it was the Lord that had given me this Truth, and a great Truth it definitely was!

After I made the statement, I paused. Loren Larson then spoke up and asked, *"Can you give me Scripture for that?"*

Since I had not studied the subject at all, when Loren asked that question, I just sat there for a brief moment. Then the Holy Spirit began to move upon me again, taking me to Romans 8:2.

As I read that Scripture, *"For the Law of the Spirit of Life in Christ Jesus has made me free from the law of sin and death,"* I knew this was the answer! I knew it was the Lord. This was the way the Holy Spirit works!

I don't recall how much time remained until the end of the Program, but I do well remember the following:

THIS IS THE FULFILLMENT OF THE PROMISE I MADE TO YOU

The Program ended, and I turned to my right, got up, and started to walk toward the door. All of a sudden, the Spirit of God once again came over me. In a flash, the Lord took me back to that March day in 1988. I saw myself standing near the fence at the back of our compound. I sensed the Presence of God greatly, exactly as I did those nine years before. I distinctly recall the Lord saying to me, *"I will show you things about the Holy Spirit you do not now know!"* As I stood there in that little Studio, the Lord spoke to my heart, *"What I have just given you, as it regards how the Holy Spirit works, is that which I promised to give you."* Again, I cannot even begin to relate how I felt. It had taken nine years, but the Lord had fulfilled exactly what He said He would do. I now knew how the Holy Spirit works in the framework of the Cross. I now knew the part which He plays, which, within itself, is an amazing Truth.

PROGRESSIVE REVELATION

As I have said so many times already, this which the Lord gave to me is not new. It was first given to the Apostle Paul, which means that what the Lord gave me was merely (if that word could be used) an enlightenment on the great Truth already given.

But yet I do believe that this simple but yet beautiful Revelation which the Lord gave to me takes the Truth of the Cross a step further than the Church has previously known. Actually, all Revelation from the Lord is progressive. In other words, when the Lord opens up something, He always opens up a Truth to a greater degree than it has heretofore been known. It does not mean it is something new, but it does mean that more understanding is given.

That's exactly what I believe the Lord has given to me. I believe it takes the great Truth of the Cross to a greater degree, a greater dimension, than the Church has previously known. Tragically, most Believers do not know or understand how the Holy Spirit works. As it regards the Denominational world, the Holy Spirit is hardly given any shift at all.

Even when it comes to Pentecostals and Charismatics, dependence on the Spirit has fallen to an alarming degree. Even in these circles, speaking with other tongues, if that, is about the limit that is known regarding the Spirit and how He works. There is a little understanding regarding *"Gifts of the Spirit,"* but as to how the Holy Spirit works in connection with Sanctification, which pertains to how we live for God, that is basically an unknown factor with the majority of the Church. And yet, that's exactly what the Lord gave to me in this Revelation.

As I've already said several times, it is not possible for me to express in words exactly how I felt when I knew that the Lord, after nine long years, had opened up to me this great Truth. He had done exactly what He said He would do! And with the Lord, whatever it is that He promises, it always is far larger than we at first realize.

Chapter 2

The Law Of The Spirit Of Life In Christ Jesus

CHAPTER TWO

THE LAW OF THE SPIRIT OF LIFE IN CHRIST JESUS

Romans 8:2 presents the two most powerful laws in the universe. They are:

1. The Law of the Spirit of Life in Christ Jesus.
2. The law of sin and death.

The only law in the universe that is stronger than the *"law of sin and death"* is the *"Law of the Spirit of Life in Christ Jesus."*

If we as Believers do not understand these two Laws, then the *"law of sin and death"* will wreak its havoc on us. Tragically, there is not one Christian out of a thousand who understands what the *"Law of the Spirit of Life in Christ Jesus"* actually is!

IT IS A LAW

The word *"Law"* is used here in connection with the Spirit of God and how He works. It actually is a *"Law"* which was devised by the Godhead sometime in eternity past (I Pet. 1:18-20). This Law is *"God's Prescribed Order of Victory."*

Since this is not only a *"Law,"* but a *"Law"* devised by the Godhead, we should understand that the Lord will never deviate from this Law. It is, therefore, incumbent upon us to know exactly what it means.

The three words, *"of the Spirit,"* actually refer to the Holy Spirit and how He works. So in this short Verse of Scripture, we are given tremendous Truths.

THE SPIRIT OF LIFE

The phrase, *"Of the Spirit of Life,"* actually tells us that everything for which Jesus paid such a price at Calvary's Cross is superintended by the Holy Spirit, which we will address more completely a little later. The Holy Spirit is in charge, and He Alone can give us what we need.

IN CHRIST JESUS

Those three words, *"In Christ Jesus,"* proclaim to us the manner in which the Law of the Spirit works. Over a hundred times in his fourteen

Epistles, the Apostle Paul uses the phrase, *"In Christ Jesus,"* or one of its derivatives, such as *"In Him"* or *"In Whom,"* etc. Without exception, it always refers to Christ, but, more particularly what He did for us at the Cross.

All of this means that our faith is to be placed exclusively in Christ and what He did for us at the Cross, which then gives the Holy Spirit latitude to work mightily within our lives, and, considering that He is God, there is nothing that He cannot do.

When we place our faith properly, the Holy Spirit will then see to it that we are *"made free from the law of sin and death."* In fact, this is the only way that victory over the *"law of sin and death"* can be effected. If we try to gain victory any other way, despite our great efforts, no victory will be forthcoming.

GOD'S PRESCRIBED ORDER OF VICTORY

The Lord has only one Prescribed Order — not ten, not five, not even two — only one. That one Prescribed Order is *"Jesus Christ and Him Crucified."*

The problem which besets the human race is the problem of *"sin."* It not only besets the unredeemed human race, but it also besets the Church. That is the primary, overwhelming problem — *"sin."* As we look at the modern Church, it becomes very obvious that it doesn't know what to do with sin. If you are in the *"Word of Faith"* camp, you are taught that sin must never be mentioned, because to do so only arouses a sin consciousness in the heart of such a person. If sin is not mentioned, that will solve the sin problem.

Nothing could be further from the truth!

The *"Purpose Driven Live"* people claim that to mention sin is offensive to people. If we remind them of sin, it might drive them away, so we just won't mention sin, because it is offensive.

To be sure, sin is most definitely offensive, but if the secret of victory over sin was simply not mentioning it, then someone should have told the Apostle Paul and all the other Bible writers. Some seventeen times in the Sixth Chapter of Romans alone the great Apostle addresses sin. He does so because that is the problem not only in the world, but also in the Church. The problem is sin!

No matter what false directions we may try to travel in our attempts to address sin, none of that will have any effect upon sin taking its deadly toll. Sin will continue to wreak havoc, breaking up homes, marriages, wrecking lives, and inflicting all sorts of other damages.

The Lord has one answer for sin, and one answer alone, because that is the only answer that is needed. The one and only answer is *"Jesus Christ and Him Crucified"* (Rom. 8:3). Sin is so awful, so bad, so terrible, and so horrible that God had to become Man, come down to this mortal coil, and give His Life on the Cross of Calvary. He did all of this in order that sin may be properly addressed, which means that it is properly cleansed and put away. It is the *"Lamb of God"* Alone which *"takes away the sin of the world"* (Jn. 1:29).

Let us say it another way:

The Lord has only one answer for sin, because there is only one answer that is needed, and that answer is the Cross of Christ. If we ignore that answer, we do so at our peril.

Let the Reader properly understand the following:

1. The only thing standing between mankind and eternal Hell is the Cross of Christ!

2. The only thing standing between the Church and total apostasy is the Cross of Christ!

If Believers do not understand this *"Law"* (and it definitely is a Law!), then Believers are going to be overcome by the *"law of sin and death,"* which will bring untold sorrow and heartache. That's what the entirety of the Seventh Chapter of Romans is all about. It pictures the Believer, in this case the Apostle Paul, attempting to live for God in all the wrong ways. Even though the Lord gave Paul the answer to this dilemma, which is the Cross of Christ, regrettably it seems that most in the modern Church are still little cognizant of this great Truth, and failure is rampant on every hand!

Chapter 3

The Cross And The Holy Spirit

CHAPTER THREE

THE CROSS AND THE HOLY SPIRIT

The Cross of Christ is the dividing line as it regards what the Holy Spirit does. It means that He worked one way before the Cross, and now works another way since the Cross.

Just before the Crucifixion, Jesus said to His Disciples, and I quote from THE EXPOSITOR'S STUDY BIBLE:

"*And I will pray the Father, and He shall give you another Comforter* ('*Parakletos,*' which means '*One called to the side of another for help*'), *that He may abide with you forever* (before the Cross, the Holy Spirit could only help a few individuals, and then only for a period of time; since the Cross, He lives in the hearts and lives of all Believers, and does so forever);

"*Even the Spirit of Truth* (the Greek says, '*The Spirit of The Truth,*' which refers to the Word of God; actually, He does far more than merely superintend the attribute of Truth, as Christ '*is Truth*' [I Jn. 5:6]); *Whom the world cannot receive* (the Holy Spirit cannot come into the heart of the unbeliever until that person makes Christ his or her Saviour; then He comes in), *because it sees Him not, neither knows Him* (refers to the fact that only Born-Again Believers can understand the Holy Spirit and know Him): *but you know Him* (would have been better translated, '*But you shall get to know Him*'); *for He dwells with you* (before the Cross), *and shall be in you* (which will take place on the Day of Pentecost and forward, because the sin debt has been forever paid by Christ on the Cross, changing the disposition of everything*") (Jn. 14:16-17).

In this Seventeenth Verse, the Lord plainly tells His Disciples that before the Cross, the Holy Spirit was "*with*" them. Since the Cross, the Holy Spirit will be "*in*" them, which, of course, began on the Day of Pentecost.

WHY WAS THE HOLY SPIRIT ONLY "*WITH*" BELIEVERS BEFORE THE CROSS INSTEAD OF "*IN*" THEM?

Animal blood, which constituted the Sacrifices, was woefully insufficient to take away sin. It served as a stop-gap measure, so to speak, which served as an atonement, but it was woefully inadequate. That is the reason the great Apostle wrote and said, "*But now* (since the Cross) *has He* (the Lord Jesus) *obtained a more excellent Ministry* (the New Covenant in Jesus' Blood is superior, and takes the place of the Old Covenant in animal blood)*, by how much also He is the Mediator of a Better Covenant* (proclaims the fact that Christ officiates between God and man according to the arrangements of the New Covenant)*, which was established upon Better Promises.* (This presents the New Covenant, explicitly based on the cleansing and forgiveness of all sin, which the Old Covenant could not do)*"* (Heb. 8:6).

Animal blood could not lift the terrible sin debt which man owed to God and could not pay. Therefore, whenever Believers before the Cross died, they were not able to go to Heaven, but rather went down into Paradise, which actually was a part of Hell, separated from the burning part only by a great gulf (Lk. 16:19-31). All Believers before the Cross actually were held captive by Satan. Due to their faith, Satan was very limited as to what he could do with them, but they still were his captives.

That's what Paul was talking about when he said, *"Wherefore He said* (Ps. 68:18)*, When He ascended up on high* (the Ascension)*, He led captivity captive* (liberated the souls in Paradise; before the Cross, despite being Believers, they were still held captive by Satan because the blood of bulls and goats could not take away the sin debt; but when Jesus died on the Cross, the sin debt was paid, and now He makes all of these His captives)*, and gave Gifts unto men.* (These *"Gifts"* include all the Attributes of Christ, all made possible by the Cross)*"* (Eph. 4:8).

So, we see that, before the Cross, Believers could not go to Heaven when they died, but rather were taken down to Paradise to await the coming completion of the Atonement on the Cross. The Holy Spirit also could not dwell within Believers on a permanent basis before the Cross.

SINCE THE CROSS

The Cross changed everything!

For one thing, the entirety of the sin debt was forever paid and settled by what Christ did at the Cross, which means that man, at least those who believe, no longer have this Sword of Damocles, so to speak, hanging over their heads.

Now, when a Believer dies, and we speak of all the time since the Cross, he immediately goes to be with the Lord in Heaven, which means that the Paradise part of Hell is now empty (Phil. 1:23).

Moreover, the Holy Spirit instantly comes into the Believer's heart and life at conversion, and will remain there forever (Jn. 14:16).

Due to the fact that the Holy Spirit abides within the hearts and lives of Believers, and does so permanently, we now have the privilege of

His leading and guidance, and on a continued basis (Jn. 16:13). As well, we also have the benefit of His Power, which is unlimited, because He is God (Acts 1:8).

Chapter 4

The Power Of God

CHAPTER FOUR

THE POWER OF GOD

Paul said, *"For the preaching of the Cross is to them who perish foolishness; but unto us which are saved it is the Power of God"* (I Cor. 1:18).

The great question is, *"How is the preaching of the Cross the Power of God?"*

First of all, there is no power in the Cross, per se. Wooden beams contain no power. Moreover, there certainly was no power in the death of Christ on the Cross, at least within itself.

In fact, Paul also said that Jesus *"was Crucified through weakness. Yet He lives by the Power of God"* (II Cor. 13:4).

While Christ most definitely died in weakness, it was a contrived weakness. In other words, He could at any time have spoken the Word and been delivered from the Cross; but, of course, if He had done that, mankind would have remained unredeemed.

So, where is the Power of which Paul spoke in I Corinthians 1:18?

The Power is in the Holy Spirit, as the Power is always in the Holy Spirit.

The idea is this:

THE CROSS MAKES IT POSSIBLE FOR
THE HOLY SPIRIT TO WORK

Whenever Jesus died on the Cross, thereby settling the sin debt forever, at least for all who will believe, this gave the Holy Spirit latitude to work within hearts and lives, which He gladly does, that is, if our faith is anchored squarely in the Cross. <u>In fact, the Holy Spirit doesn't demand much of us, but He does demand that our faith be exclusively in Christ and what Christ has done for us at the Cross</u> (Rom. 6:1-14).

Therefore, when the Preacher *"preaches the Cross,"* with Believers thereby placing their faith exclusively in Christ and the Cross, this gives the Holy Spirit latitude to work, thereby exhibiting His Power, which is Almighty. This is the only way for the Believer to live a victorious, overcoming Christian Life. This is the Way the Holy Spirit works, and we continue to speak of Christ and the Cross.

Let us say it again:

While Christ is always the Source, the Cross is always the Means. All of this means that the Power of God cannot be exhibited except by and through the Means of the Cross. It is the Cross of Christ which has made everything possible; that includes Salvation, the Baptism with the Holy Spirit, Sanctification, the Gifts of the Spirit, the Fruit of the Spirit, answered prayer in every capacity, and blessings of all dimensions. It is all by and through the Cross!

Because it is so very, very important, please allow us to say it even one more time:

**THE HOLY SPIRIT ALONE CAN MAKE US
WHAT WE OUGHT TO BE**

The greatest bane of the modern Church is Believers who have been saved by <u>Faith</u> and now attempt to effect Sanctification by <u>self</u>. It was the bane of the Church during Paul's day, which provoked him to write his very strong Epistle to the Galatians; it also is the problem presently.

Chapter 5

Outside Of The Cross There Is Nothing But Bondage!

CHAPTER FIVE

OUTSIDE OF THE CROSS THERE IS NOTHING BUT BONDAGE!

The great Fifth Chapter of Galatians proclaims what happens to the Believer who tries to function outside of the Cross, which means that he is functioning without the help of the Holy Spirit.

In the dissertation given in this Fifth Chapter, we are also told how to *"walk in the Spirit."* We will take it Verse by Verse.

(1) "STAND FAST THEREFORE IN THE LIBERTY WHEREWITH CHRIST HAS MADE US FREE, AND BE NOT ENTANGLED AGAIN WITH THE YOKE OF BONDAGE."

The *"liberty"* addressed here has to do with liberty to live a Godly Christian Life. Without understanding the Cross, one does not have that liberty, and cannot thereby function in such liberty, and will thereby conclude in bondage of some nature.

What Jesus did at the Cross has *"made us free,"* and what Jesus did at the Cross alone has made us free. We must never forget that. It is not so much the Church we attend, or anything else, which has made us free, even though those things may be very important. It is what Christ has done for us at the Cross, and that alone.

Paul had founded the Churches in Galatia; consequently, they had been brought in right. In other words, they had been privileged to have the greatest teaching on the face of the Earth, that from the great Apostle himself; however, after he left and went on to other fields of endeavor, false apostles came in and taught that one had to also keep the Law in order to be saved, etc.

We may wonder as to how the Believers in these Churches in Galatia, especially considering that they had been privileged to have the greatest teaching in the world, would have fallen for such false doctrine.

DECEPTION

False doctrine carries its own power. It is freighted with deception, deceiving the hearer, because it is meant to deceive. Deception is, no doubt, Satan's greatest weapon. Millions are in Hell today, and millions more are on their way to Hell because of the one problem and power of deception.

Moreover, there is something about the human being, even a Godly person, which desires to *"do something"* to effect one's own Righteousness and Holiness. We like to think that we have done something, that we have merited something, that we have contributed something toward that which we have. But, truthfully, we have not!

It is all in Christ, for He Alone has *"made us free."*

ENTANGLEMENT

The phrase, *"And be not entangled again with the yoke of bondage,"* plainly says that if the Believer leaves the Message of Christ and the Cross, then whatever direction that Believer takes, the end result will be *"bondage."*

What do we mean by bondage?

We are referring to the fact that such a Believer no longer has liberty to live a holy life. He is in bondage to a work or lust of the flesh, which will get worse and worse. The only way that one can rid oneself of such entanglement is to repent of their actions, whatever those actions might be, and thereby once again place their faith exclusively in Christ and what Christ has done at the Cross.

It is sad, but the far greater majority of the modern Church truly is *"entangled in bondage,"* simply because they do not understand the Cross, as it regards Sanctification.

(2) "BEHOLD, I PAUL SAY UNTO YOU, THAT IF YOU BE CIRCUMCISED, CHRIST SHALL PROFIT YOU NOTHING."

When Paul uses the type of statement he did, *"I Paul say unto you,"* he is presenting his Apostolic authority as it regarded the Message he was bringing.

He is saying that if the Galatians (or anyone else, for that matter) ignore what he is saying, they will do so at their peril. The reason is simple: what he is saying is the Word of the Lord.

I can make the same statement regarding these words which I am writing, simply because they are not my words. They are straight from the Word of God.

If the Believer ignores the Cross, thereby subscribing to something else, pure and simple, *"Christ shall profit you nothing."*

Paul used the analogy here of *"circumcision,"* which was the physical symbol of the Old Covenant. The problem was this:

These false teachers were telling the Galatians that in order to be the kind of Christian they should be, they not only had to accept Christ, but the men and the little boys also had to be circumcised. So Paul tells the Galatians that if they submit to such erroneous teaching, all that Christ did at the Cross will serve no purpose whatsoever.

Even though *"circumcision"* is not the emphasis now, still, the principle is the same. If the Believer places his faith and trust in his Church, in a Preacher, in his good works, in the money that he gives, or in speaking with other tongues, or in Water Baptism, or a host a other things which could be mentioned, many of which are very good, still, if one's faith is in any of those things, *"Christ shall profit you nothing."*

That is a very somber statement, and one that should be inspected very closely. It means that what Christ did at the Cross will be of absolutely no avail to the person who places his faith in something other than the Cross. Regrettably, most of the modern Church falls into that category. As a consequence, *"Christ profits them nothing."*

Please allow me to say it again:

If our faith is in anything except Christ and the Cross, irrespective as to what the *"anything"* might be, we have just forfeited Christ and all He accomplished for us at the Cross. That should be a very sober statement!

(3) "FOR I TESTIFY AGAIN TO EVERY MAN WHO IS CIRCUMCISED, THAT HE IS A DEBTOR TO DO THE WHOLE LAW."

The Believer has only one of two ways that he can go. It is *"Law"* or *"Grace."* It cannot be both!

Most modern Believers would blanch at the thought of *"Law,"* claiming that they are not serving or trusting in any type of Law.

Let us say it again:

If one's faith is not absolutely in Christ and the Cross, then the only other place for one to be, whether they understand it or not, is *"Law."* As stated, there are only two roads on this landscape, and those roads are *"Law"* and *"Grace."*

The far greater majority of the modern Church understands nothing at all about the Cross of Christ, as it regards Sanctification. This automatically means that the modern Church, even if by default, is basically trying to function in Law, whether they understand it or not.

Chapter 6

Fallen From Grace

CHAPTER SIX

FALLEN FROM GRACE

(4) "CHRIST IS BECOME OF NO EFFECT UNTO YOU, WHO-SOEVER OF YOU ARE JUSTIFIED BY THE LAW; YOU ARE FALLEN FROM GRACE."

The statement, *"Christ shall profit you nothing,"* is now joined by the statement, *"Christ is become of no effect unto you."* Both mean the same thing. To be frank, these are chilling statements, but they characterize most of modern Christianity.

Millions presently are attempting to be justified by *"Law,"* i.e., *"works."* Let it ever be understood, this is justification that God will not recognize. He recognizes only one type of Justification, and that is Faith that we have in Christ and what Christ has done for us at the Cross. Such Faith will always guarantee a 100% justification, which is the only type of Justification that God will recognize.

What does it mean to fall from Grace?

It has the very opposite meaning from what most people think.

Most Christians think that if one sins, they have fallen from Grace.

If that is the case, then every single Believer on the face of the Earth has fallen from Grace, for, at one time or another, every single Believer has sinned.

Some time ago, I was listening to a group of Preachers over Television discussing this very subject. Their consensus was that if someone committed sins, or certain types of sins, then they were *"fallen from Grace."*

To be frank, that's the very person who needs the Grace of God!

No! Falling from Grace is not committing sin, as dastardly and as awful as that is. It is rather someone placing their faith in other than Christ and the Cross. Tragically and sadly, that being the case, this means that almost all of the modern Church has fallen from Grace.

Please understand: What I have just stated is exactly what the Apostle Paul is telling the Galatians, and all else concerned for that matter.

GRACE

The Grace of God is simply the Goodness of God extended to undeserving Believers. It is the Cross which makes the Grace of God possible — and nothing else, we might quickly add!

God has no more Grace today than He did three thousand years ago. God doesn't change. What He was then, He is now. It is the Cross which has opened up the gate, so to speak.

To be sure, every single thing that any Believer has ever received from the Lord at any time has always been by and through the Grace of God. God cannot bestow good things on us in any other fashion, simply because it is not possible to earn that which He Alone can give.

But before the Cross, since animal blood was woefully insufficient, the Lord was limited as to what He could do regarding *"Grace."* Since the Cross, there are no limits, at least no limits on what the Lord may do. To be sure, we greatly limit the Lord regarding the Grace He can bestow, simply because we at times *"frustrate the Grace of God"* (Gal. 2:20-21).

Everything, including the Grace of God, comes to us strictly through the Cross of Christ. As we have repeatedly stated, and continue to state, *"Christ is the Source, and the Cross is the Means."* If our faith is elsewhere, irrespective as to where that *"elsewhere"* might be, pure and simple, the Holy Spirit through the Apostle says, *"You are fallen from Grace."*

To be sure, that puts the Believer in an extremely precarious situation.

(5) "FOR WE THROUGH THE SPIRIT WAIT FOR THE HOPE OF RIGHTEOUSNESS BY FAITH."

This Verse of Scripture has two meanings:

First of all, it speaks of the coming Resurrection of Life, which will take place at the Trump of God (I Thess. 4:13-18).

The second meaning may be even more important, which refers to Believers at the present time.

Once the Believer places his faith in Christ and the Cross, this does not mean that Satan will instantly cease all activity against such a Believer, and that it will be nothing but smooth sailing from here on out. Satan will never let up. He will continue to try to hinder, and he will take advantage of the Believer's lapses of faith.

Our faith never is quite as strong as we think it is. Satan takes advantage of that. But Paul is telling us here that *"we through the Spirit,"* which speaks of the Holy Spirit and His Work within our lives, must *"wait for the Hope of Righteousness,"* and do so *"by Faith."* In other words, with our Faith now in Christ and the Cross, we must understand that now we are on the right path. Even though there may be some ups and downs on this path, and even some failures, still, we are guaranteed that ultimately *"sin shall not have dominion over us"* (Rom. 6:14). We have this *"hope,"* and it is a *"Hope of Righteousness."* It is gained *"by Faith,"* which refers to Faith in Christ and what Christ did at the Cross.

**SELF-HELP
STUDY NOTES**

(6) "FOR IN JESUS CHRIST NEITHER CIRCUMCISION AVAILS ANYTHING NOR UNCIRCUMCISION; BUT FAITH WHICH WORKS BY LOVE."

Paul is telling the Galatians here that whether they are circumcised or not has no bearing on anything they do or anything they are, as it regards the Lord. It is the same thing with every kind of *"work"* in which one participates. But yet, most of the modern Church ignores this Passage.

How do I know that?

Many think that their association with a certain Church affords them some type of spirituality. Millions think that their good works account for something. Others think that their endeavoring to keep Commandments surely avails them something!

Let all and sundry understand that these things avail nothing. It is rather *"by Faith,"* which always *"works by Love."*

Law, i.e., *"works,"* always breeds self-righteousness. In a sense, it nurtures and fosters hate in the hearts of its participants. True Faith in the Lord *"works by love"* and generates love.

It goes all the way back to Cain and Abel. There is no difference between the brothers, but an eternal difference between their sacrifices. They are both corrupt branches of a decayed tree, both born outside Eden, both guilty, both sinners, no moral difference, and both sentenced to death.

The Lord had a way that Abel accepted, but which Cain rejected. Abel's way, rather the Lord's, was the Altar, which spoke of Repentance, of Faith, and of the Precious Blood of Christ, the Lamb of God without blemish. Cain's altar tells of pride, unbelief, and self-righteousness; consequently, he murdered his brother.

Abel's Altar is beautiful to God's Eye and repulsive to man's. Cain's Altar, beautiful to man's eye and repulsive to God's. These *"altars"* exist today; around the one, that is, Christ and His Atoning Work, few are gathered; around the other, many. God accepts the slain lamb and rejects the offered fruit; the offering being rejected, so, of necessity, is the offerer.

It has not changed at the present time. The Lord doesn't look at the sacrificer; He looks solely at the Sacrifice. If the Sacrifice is accepted, then the sacrificer is accepted.

The Church does not readily accept such. The Church loves its *"works."*

But let the Reader understand the following:

"Love" is generated by True Faith; it is never generated by works. For Faith to be true, it must rest, without fail, in Christ and the Cross, and in nothing else!

(7) "YOU DID RUN WELL; WHO DID HINDER YOU THAT YOU SHOULD NOT OBEY THE TRUTH?"

That question also could be asked of the modern Church!

What is the Truth which Paul is exclaiming? It is the Truth of Jesus Christ and Him Crucified as the sole means of Salvation and Sanctification. The Galatians were falling away from this Truth and were accepting other things.

Paul's statement about them *"running well"* refers to what he had taught them and how they had been brought into the Gospel. Now they were listening to other voices, and the truth was falling by the wayside.

Let me say it again:

The Gospel is very simple. It is the story of Jesus Christ and what He has done for us as it regards Redemption, which refers to the Cross. Pure and simple, that is the *"Truth."* If anything else is accepted, irrespective as to what it might be, or how good it may look on the surface, a disobedience to the Truth is the result, and the end of that is disaster.

(8) "THIS PERSUASION COMES NOT OF HIM WHO CALLS YOU."

Paul is telling the Galatians and all other Believers (and for all time) that their foray into false doctrine did not come about because of a Moving and Leading of the Holy Spirit. The Holy Spirit doesn't change His Mind. So, the *"persuasion"* they had experienced had come from these false teachers, which means the direction was not, and is not, of God.

**HOW COULD THESE GALATIANS BE PERSUADED
TO DEPART FROM THAT TAUGHT BY PAUL?**

Deception is a powerful force, and, to be sure, all false doctrine is always coupled with the spirit of deception (I Tim. 4:1).

These Galatians had had the greatest teacher in the world, namely, the Apostle Paul. What they had been taught was exactly what the Holy Spirit wanted to be taught. It was taught under the anointing of the Holy Spirit and had resulted in changed lives. But now these false apostles had come in and were teaching Law to the Galatians. Regrettably, some were accepting what they were hearing, i.e., they were being *"persuaded."*

(9) "A LITTLE LEAVEN LEAVENS THE WHOLE LUMP."

The introduction of a small amount of false doctrine will ultimately consume the entirety of the belief system.

LEAVEN

The Holy Spirit uses *"leaven"* in the Bible as a metaphor for spiritual corruption. In the natural, leaven is that which instigates fermentation. It is what turns grape juice into alcoholic beverage. So the Holy Spirit uses the word to explain the rot or corruption of false doctrine which is inserted into the true Message.

The results?

The good doctrine does not finally bring the bad doctrine into the right way. The opposite is the result. The false doctrine corrupts the whole.

It is like putting one rotten apple into a barrel of good apples. The good apples will not heal the bad apple; the bad apple will, if allowed to remain, rather corrupt the entirety of the barrel.

FALSE DOCTRINE

That is the reason that all false doctrine must be identified and addressed. The thought that false doctrine will simply go away if it is ignored is erroneous, as this Scripture confirms. If the *"little leaven"* is not rooted out, it will corrupt the whole. That means that true Preachers of the Gospel must point out false doctrine, must call attention to false doctrine, and must label it as exactly what it is, even as Paul is doing here.

My son Donnie made a statement the other day that I believe bears repeating. In one of his Messages, he said:

"If Preachers point out false doctrine, and do not put a name or a face to the false doctrine, most Christians will applaud such action; however, if the false doctrine is pointed out and a name and a face are attached to that false doctrine, i.e., if the name of the Preacher who is preaching the false doctrine is identified, then many people grow angry."

Why would they applaud an action in one case and grow angry in the other?

Such attitude and action shows that the emphasis is not really on the Truth, but rather on a person. If they like a person who is preaching false doctrine, then they think the false doctrine is satisfactory.

The emphasis for every Believer should not be the person, but rather the Truth. Is what is being said the Truth, or is what being said false? That, and that alone, is the question!

(10) "I HAVE CONFIDENCE IN YOU THROUGH THE LORD, THAT YOU WILL BE NONE OTHERWISE MINDED: BUT HE WHO TROUBLES YOU SHALL BEAR HIS JUDGMENT, WHOSOEVER HE BE."

Paul is saying two things here:

1. He is saying that those who are proclaiming this false doctrine, which pertains to attempting to draw the Galatians away from Grace to Law, would prove to be a great trouble to those who adhered to this false message.

2. The Apostle is saying that *"judgment"* is definitely going to come upon those who preach such false doctrine. It may not come immediately, but ultimately it shall! This refers to those who would attempt to present a way of salvation and sanctification other than Christ and the Cross.

TROUBLE

False doctrine is always presented in such a light that it seems to be accurate and truthful. But without exception, if one follows any false doctrine, it will cause trouble — and great trouble, at that!

That's the reason that this Ministry stands up against the modern fads, such as *"The Purpose Driven Life," "The Word of Faith,"* etc., because we know the end result will not be pleasant or pretty. The end result will be *"trouble"* with a capital *"T."* It cannot be otherwise! Trouble may or may not come quickly, but come it shall!

(11) "AND I, BRETHREN, IF I YET PREACH CIRCUMCISION, WHY DO I YET SUFFER PERSECUTION? THEN IS THE OFFENSE OF THE CROSS CEASED."

Any message other than the Cross draws little opposition.

THE OFFENSE OF THE CROSS

Why is the Cross of Christ an offense?

What did Paul mean by this statement, considering that the Cross actually is the emblem, so to speak, of the Church?

The Cross may be the emblem of the Church, but, with most, that's all it is — just an emblem. The true meaning of the Cross is little known; and, when it is known, many times it is rejected.

Why?

The Message of the Cross destroys all human endeavor and human ability. In other words, it is the biggest threat to the *"flesh."* And, to be sure, man, especially religious man, places great stock in his *"works."* The Cross condemns all of that, throwing it out, making it of no effect whatsoever.

This means that it is very hard for religious man to admit that all of his doings, all of his efforts, and all of his works, whatever they might be, are thrown out. They are of no use; they are of no benefit! As stated, this does not set well at all.

In view of this, the Cross tells man, even showing him in glaring detail, how helpless he is, while, at the same time, proclaiming the total victory which Christ carried out for us at the Cross. Man does not enjoy being placed in such a helpless position. But that's what the Cross does!

Man shouts, *"Do!"* The Cross shouts, *"Done!"* That leaves man with only the faculty of faith.

(12) "I WOULD THEY WERE EVEN CUT OFF WHICH TROUBLE YOU."

The Apostle Paul is saying that he wishes that all of these Preachers who are preaching the *"Purpose Driven Life"* doctrine, or the *"Word of Faith"* doctrine, or a host of other false doctrines, were *"cut off,"* i.e., *"shown to be what they really are."* But, regrettably, that is not now the case. To be sure, however, one day it definitely shall be. That will happen when Jesus comes back!

Chapter 7

Liberty

CHAPTER SEVEN

LIBERTY

(13) "FOR, BRETHREN, YOU HAVE BEEN CALLED UNTO LIBERTY; ONLY USE NOT LIBERTY FOR AN OCCASION TO THE FLESH, BUT BY LOVE SERVE ONE ANOTHER."

The liberty addressed here refers to *"liberty from the Law, liberty to live a Holy Life."*

The Lord did not call individuals to keep rules and regulations. That is not the idea of Bible Christianity. Our *"liberty"* is in Christ and Christ Alone. It is brought about by the Believer evidencing Faith in Christ and what Christ has done at the Cross. This is the only true liberty there is; actually it is liberty unexcelled!

LIBERTY AS AN OCCASION FOR THE FLESH?

When Paul made the statement, *"Only use not liberty for an occasion to the flesh,"* what did the Apostle mean? He is saying that just because we have *"liberty,"* which is found in Christ, which means that we are not bound by rules, Commandments, laws, and rituals, etc., still, it doesn't mean that we are to look at sin with impunity.

The Believer is ever to understand that any foray into sin will bring disastrous consequences. This *"liberty"* of which Paul speaks, which is found only in Christ and what He has done for us at the Cross, is the only direction that actually will keep one from sinning. Everything else will lead to sin and failure. It is only Faith in the Cross which affords liberty, which gives one the ability to live a Holy life.

LOVE

The phrase, *"But by love serve one another,"* tells us that the moment one goes into law-keeping or ritual Christianity, love goes out the window. The only way that love can be developed in the heart and life of the Believer is for that Believer's faith to be properly placed. We continue to speak of Christ and the Cross.

The reason there is so little love in the modern Church is because the Cross has been delegated to obscurity. Without the Cross, Christianity becomes a hollow shell.

(14) "FOR ALL THE LAW IS FULFILLED IN ONE WORD, EVEN IN THIS; YOU SHALL LOVE YOUR NEIGHBOR AS YOURSELF."

In this last phrase, the whole Law stands fully obeyed. This can be done, and this will be done, providing the Believer ever makes the Cross of Christ the Object of his Faith. Accordingly, the Holy Spirit will then provide the Power for us to do what we should do.

(15) "BUT IF YOU BITE AND DEVOUR ONE ANOTHER, TAKE HEED THAT YOU BE NOT CONSUMED ONE OF ANOTHER."

If love is absent, this tells us that the Cross is absent. Biting and quarreling always follow the Law.

Chapter 8

Walking In The Spirit

CHAPTER EIGHT

WALKING IN THE SPIRIT

(16) "THIS I SAY THEN, WALK IN THE SPIRIT, AND YOU SHALL NOT FULFILL THE LUST OF THE FLESH."

The word *"walk"* is used by Paul in the sense of the manner in which one orders his behavior. As Believers, we are to *"walk in the Spirit,"* which refers to placing our faith solely in Christ and the Cross, through which the Spirit exclusively works (Rom. 8:1-2).

Many people think that *"walking in the Spirit"* has to do with doing spiritual things, such as faithful attendance to Church, giving money to the work of the Lord, witnessing to souls, etc. Those things definitely are desirable and commendable, and are things that any good Christian will do; however, that is not what *"walking in the Spirit"* actually means.

The manner in which the Spirit operates, which is what this Study Guide is all about, pertains to Christ and what Christ did at the Cross. We are to place our faith exclusively in the Finished Work of our Lord, and maintain our faith in that Finished Work, even on a daily basis (Lk. 9:23). That is what the Spirit demands of us, and that is what constitutes *"walking in the Spirit."*

THE SIN NATURE

The phrase, *"And you shall not fulfill the lust of the flesh,"* proves the existence of the sin nature in the Believer. (Please see our Study Guide on the Sin Nature.)

The *"lust of the flesh"* proclaims the consciousness of corrupt desires. There is only one way to throttle the sin nature, so to speak, and that is to *"walk in the Spirit,"* which, as stated, refers to our faith being placed exclusively in Christ and the Cross.

The *"sin nature"* is the state of all of humanity as a result of the Fall. Every individual is given over to sin, to doing wrong, to disobeying God. In fact, every unsaved person is ruled and controlled totally and completely by the sin nature.

As we see here, Christians will also be ruled by the sin nature, i.e., *"the lust of the flesh,"* if their faith is placed in anything except Christ and the Cross. If it is, Paul stated that *"Christ shall profit you nothing."*

This is the area where the Believer has his greatest problem. Regrettably and sadly, most Christians have very little knowledge about how to over-come in this area. Consequently, it is quite common to hear every type of scheme that one can contemplate being projected as the answer to the sin problem. There is only one answer to the sin problem, and that is the Cross of Christ.

(17) "FOR THE FLESH LUSTS AGAINST THE SPIRIT, AND THE SPIRIT AGAINST THE FLESH: AND THESE ARE CONTRARY THE ONE TO THE OTHER: SO THAT YOU CANNOT DO THE THINGS THAT YOU WOULD."

Paul uses the word *"walk"* fairly consistently, and he also uses the word *"flesh"* over and over again. *"Flesh"* speaks of the Believer's personal prowess, ability, personal strength, etc. Within themselves, these things are not wrong; however, they become wrong when we try to use them to live for God, which is mostly the way the majority of the Church attempts to live.

There is a constant conflict going on between the *"flesh"* and the *"Spirit,"* speaking of the Holy Spirit. If the *"flesh"* attempts to chart the course, which it definitely will do if the Believer does not understand the Cross, then the Holy Spirit will be greatly hindered in His help to us.

We must understand that it is the Holy Spirit Alone Who can subdue the flesh; He Alone can make us what we ought to be. No matter how strong in the Lord we might be, or think to be, we cannot bring about in our lives that which must be. Only the Holy Spirit can do that!

We must remember that the Holy Spirit works exclusively within the framework of the Finished Work of Christ. He will function in no other manner (Rom. 8:2). As a consequence, He demands that we place our faith exclusively in Christ and the Cross, and leave it there, which then gives Him the latitude to work in our lives. It is, however, a struggle for us to not depend on the flesh. This is the most difficult thing for the Believer to do, and I speak of arresting the flesh.

We must ever realize that the direction the flesh desires to take, no matter how religious it might be, is always *"contrary to the Holy Spirit."*

The phrase, *"So that you cannot do the things that you would,"* simply means that it is impossible for the Believer to live a victorious and overcoming Christian Life if the Believer doesn't place his faith exclusively in Christ and the Cross.

(18) "BUT IF YOU BE LED OF THE SPIRIT, YOU ARE NOT UNDER THE LAW."

One cannot follow the Spirit and the Law at the same time. Regrettably, that, however, is what most modern Christians are attempting to do. Unless one properly understands the Cross as it regards Sanctification, one cannot be properly *"led of the Spirit,"* Who works exclusively within the framework of the Finished Work of Christ.

THE WORKS OF THE FLESH

(19) "NOW THE WORKS OF THE FLESH ARE MANIFEST, WHICH ARE THESE; ADULTERY, FORNICATION, UNCLEANNESS, LASCIVIOUSNESS,

(20) "IDOLATRY, WITCHCRAFT, HATRED, VARIANCE, EMULATIONS, WRATH, STRIFE, SEDITIONS, HERESIES,

(21) "ENVYINGS, MURDERS, DRUNKENNESS, REVELLINGS, AND SUCH LIKE: OF THE WHICH I TELL YOU BEFORE, AS I HAVE ALSO TOLD YOU IN TIME PAST, THAT THEY WHICH DO SUCH THINGS SHALL NOT INHERIT THE KINGDOM OF GOD."

If one is walking after the flesh (Rom. 8:1), one or more of these sins will manifest themselves in one's life; the only way (and I mean the only way!) that one can walk in perpetual victory is to understand that everything we receive from God comes to us by means of the Cross; consequently, the Cross must ever be the Object of our Faith. When this is the case, the Holy Spirit, Who works exclusively within the confines of the Sacrifice of Christ, will exert His mighty Power on our behalf, which will enable us to live a Holy life.

As is obvious here, the Apostle was not afraid to name particular sins.

In no uncertain terms, the last phrase of this Verse plainly tells us that if our faith is not everlastingly in Christ and the Cross, we simply won't make it. God doesn't have two ways of Salvation and Victory. He only has one, which is *"Jesus Christ and Him Crucified."*

Chapter 9

Fruit Of The Spirit

CHAPTER NINE

FRUIT OF THE SPIRIT

(22) "BUT THE FRUIT OF THE SPIRIT IS LOVE, JOY, PEACE, LONGSUFFERING, GENTLENESS, GOODNESS, FAITH,

(23) "MEEKNESS, TEMPERANCE: AGAINST SUCH THERE IS NO LAW."

The *"Fruit of the Spirit"* can be developed in our lives only by the Holy Spirit, inasmuch as it is His Fruit.

Again, He does such, which is the great Work that must be carried out in the heart and life of every Believer, strictly on the basis of the Finished Work of Christ.

In other words, there is no way that you and I can develop this Fruit in our lives. To be sure, it can be developed, but the Holy Spirit Alone must do such. As we have repeatedly stated, everything He does is done exclusively within the framework of the Sacrifice of Christ. It only requires Faith on our part, meaning that we ever make the Cross the Object of our Faith.

(24) "AND THEY WHO ARE CHRIST'S HAVE CRUCIFIED THE FLESH WITH THE AFFECTIONS AND LUSTS."

This can be done only by the Believer understanding that it was carried out by Christ at the Cross, and our being *"baptized into His Death"* (Rom. 6:3-5). The Cross must ever be the Object of our Faith, which alone will bring about these results.

(25) "IF WE LIVE IN THE SPIRIT, LET US ALSO WALK IN THE SPIRIT."

"Walk" refers to our lifestyle; this Passage declares both life and holiness to be the Work of the Holy Spirit. He operates Salvation and He operates Sanctification; both are realized on the principle of Faith, and that refers to the Cross ever being the Object of our Faith. Many know they have received Spiritual Life as it regards Salvation through Faith, but they think they can only secure Sanctification by works. This is a great error, which never brings victory. Believing in Christ and the Cross for Sanctification (as well as for Justification) introduces one into a life of Power and

Victory, which is the only way it can be accomplished.

(26) "LET US NOT BE DESIROUS OF VAIN GLORY, PRO-VOKING ONE ANOTHER, ENVYING ONE ANOTHER."

If vain glory is present, this is a sign that one is functioning according to Law, and not according to Grace.

This last Verse of this Chapter tells us what will happen if we place our faith in anything except Christ and the Cross. Doing such greatly hinders the Holy Spirit.

In this Study Guide, we have done our best to open up to you, the Reader, the means by which the Holy Spirit works. I trust we have made it abundantly clear that He operates exclusively within the framework of the Cross of Christ (Rom. 6:1-14; 8:1-2, 11; I Cor. 1:17-18, 21, 23; 2:2; Gal. 6:14).

If the Believer will ever exhibit simple Faith, with the Object of that Faith being Christ and the Cross, the Holy Spirit will then be able to carry out within our lives that which He Alone can do. This is God's Prescribed Order of Victory, and His only Prescribed Order of Victory. He has no other, because He needs no other!

Chapter 10

The Lamb And The Holy Spirit

CHAPTER TEN

THE LAMB AND THE HOLY SPIRIT

As I conclude the material regarding this Study Guide on the Holy Spirit and how He works, I think there could be no greater portrayal than a short synopsis of John the Beloved's Vision of the Throne of God.

John said, and I quote from THE EXPOSITOR'S STUDY BIBLE:

THE SEALED BOOK

"And I saw in the Right Hand (signifies power) *of Him Who sat on the Throne a Book written within and on the backside, sealed with Seven Seals.* (The *'Seven Seals'* signify that the *'Time of Jacob's Trouble'* is about to begin, which will rapidly bring to a conclusion that which must be done.)

"And I saw a strong Angel proclaiming with a loud voice (this strong Angel is probably Gabriel, as evidenced by Gabriel's appearance to Daniel), *Who is worthy to open the Book, and to loose the Seals thereof?* (This implies moral fitness [Rom. 1:4].)

"And no man in Heaven, nor in Earth, neither under the Earth, was able to open the Book, neither to look thereon. (We should look very carefully at the words *'no man.'*)

"And I wept much, because no man was found worthy to open and to read the Book, neither to look thereon. (This pertains to the fact that this Book is so very, very important. It contains not only the information regarding the coming Judgment upon this Earth, but as well the message that this Judgment, as tendered by God, will ultimately lead to the Redemption of the Earth.)

THE LION AND THE LAMB

"And one of the Elders said unto me, Weep not (states that man's dilemma has been solved)*: behold, the Lion of the Tribe of Judah, the Root of David, has prevailed to open the Book, and to loose the Seven Seals thereof* (presents Jesus Christ).

"And I beheld, and, lo, in the midst of the Throne and of the four Beasts, and in the midst of the Elders, stood a Lamb as it had been slain (the Crucifixion of Christ is represented here by the word *"Lamb,"* which refers to the fact that it was the Cross which redeemed mankind;

73

the slain Lamb Alone has redeemed all things), *having seven horns* (horns denote dominion, and *"seven"* denotes total dominion; all of this was done for you and me, meaning that we can have total dominion over the powers of darkness, and in every capacity; so there is no excuse for a lack of victory) *and seven eyes* (denotes total, perfect, pure, and complete illumination of all things spiritual, which is again made possible for you and me by the Cross; if the Believer makes the Cross the Object of his Faith, he will never be drawn away by false doctrine), *which are the Seven Spirits of God sent forth into all the Earth* (signifying that the Holy Spirit, in all His Perfection and universality, functions entirely within the parameters of the Finished Work of Christ; in other words, it is required that we ever make the Cross the Object of our Faith, which gives the Holy Spirit latitude, and guarantees the *"dominion"* and the *"illumination"* [Isa. 11:2; Rom. 8:2]).

"And He (the Lord Jesus Christ) *came and took the Book out of the Right Hand of Him* (God the Father) *Who sat upon the Throne.* (All of Heaven stands in awe as the Lamb steps forward to take the Book") (Rev. 5:1-7).

THE PROXIMITY OF THE HOLY SPIRIT TO THE LAMB OF GOD

The idea of this Passage is:

One of the Elders proclaimed the fact that the *"Lion of the Tribe of Judah, the Root of David"* was worthy to open the Book.

But when John looked toward the Throne of God, he instead *"saw a Lamb as it had been slain."*

What is the moral of this?

The moral is that we cannot have Christ as the *"Lion"* until we first accept Him as *"Lamb."* Unfortunately, many are attempting to bypass the Cross, which this illustration tells us cannot be done.

Then John describes the Holy Spirit as having *"seven horns and seven eyes, which are the Seven Spirits of God sent forth into all the Earth."*

The idea of this Passage is that the Holy Spirit and the *"slain Lamb"* are so closely intertwined that they are inseparable. All of this tells us that the Holy Spirit works entirely within the framework of the Finished Work of Christ, a statement which we have made over and over again in this Study Guide.

When the term *"Seven Spirits"* is used, it is not meaning that there are seven Holy Spirits. Rather, it refers to the seven attributes of the Holy Spirit. Those attributes are listed in Isaiah. They are:

1. The Spirit of the Lord.

2. The Spirit of Wisdom.
3. The Spirit of Understanding.
4. The Spirit of Counsel.
5. The Spirit of Might.
6. The Spirit of Knowledge.
7. The Spirit of the Fear of the Lord (Isa. 11:2).

All of this is available to the Child of God, and is meant to be available to the Child of God; however, for the Believer to avail himself of these great attributes, proper faith must be employed, and we speak of the Cross of Christ ever being the Object of one's Faith.

The *"slain Lamb"* has given the Holy Spirit the legal right to carry out His great Work in our lives. It only requires faith on our part.

Once again, we go back to Romans:

"For the Law of the Spirit of Life in Christ Jesus has made me free from the law of sin and death" (Rom. 8:2).